John Williams

# FROGS

Illustrated by

Jackie Harland

Language Consultant:
*Diana Bentley*
*University of Reading*

PUFFIN BOOKS

**Notes for parents and teachers**
This book has been specially written and designed as a first natural history book. For beginner readers there are introductory captions, while the more detailed text explains each illustration.

Words in **bold** type are explained in the glossary on p.31.

# Contents

# The story of a frog.

Here are two adult frogs in a pond. Did you know that frogs can live on the land and in the water? A frog is a kind of animal called an **amphibian**. An amphibian always begins its life in water.

# The female frog lays hundreds of eggs in the water.

The male frog holds the female to **mate** with her. As she lays the eggs he covers them with a liquid from his body. The liquid is called **sperm**. Now the eggs can begin to grow. They stick together and we call this **frogspawn**.

# Each egg grows inside a ball of jelly.

The frogspawn floats on the top of the pond. Soon the eggs start to change shape. After seven days they have almost changed into **tadpoles**. Can you see how the head and tail have grown inside the jelly ball?

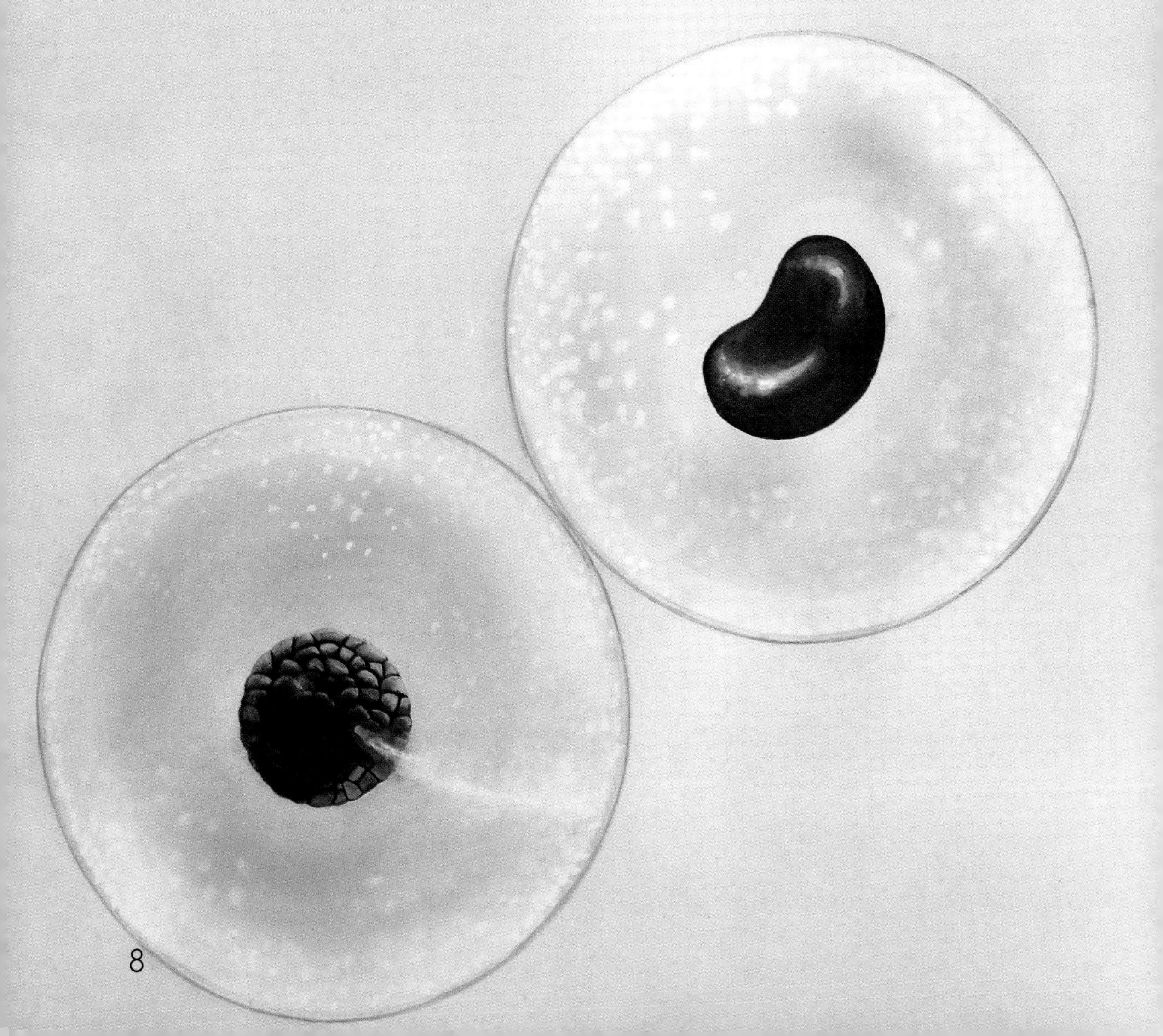

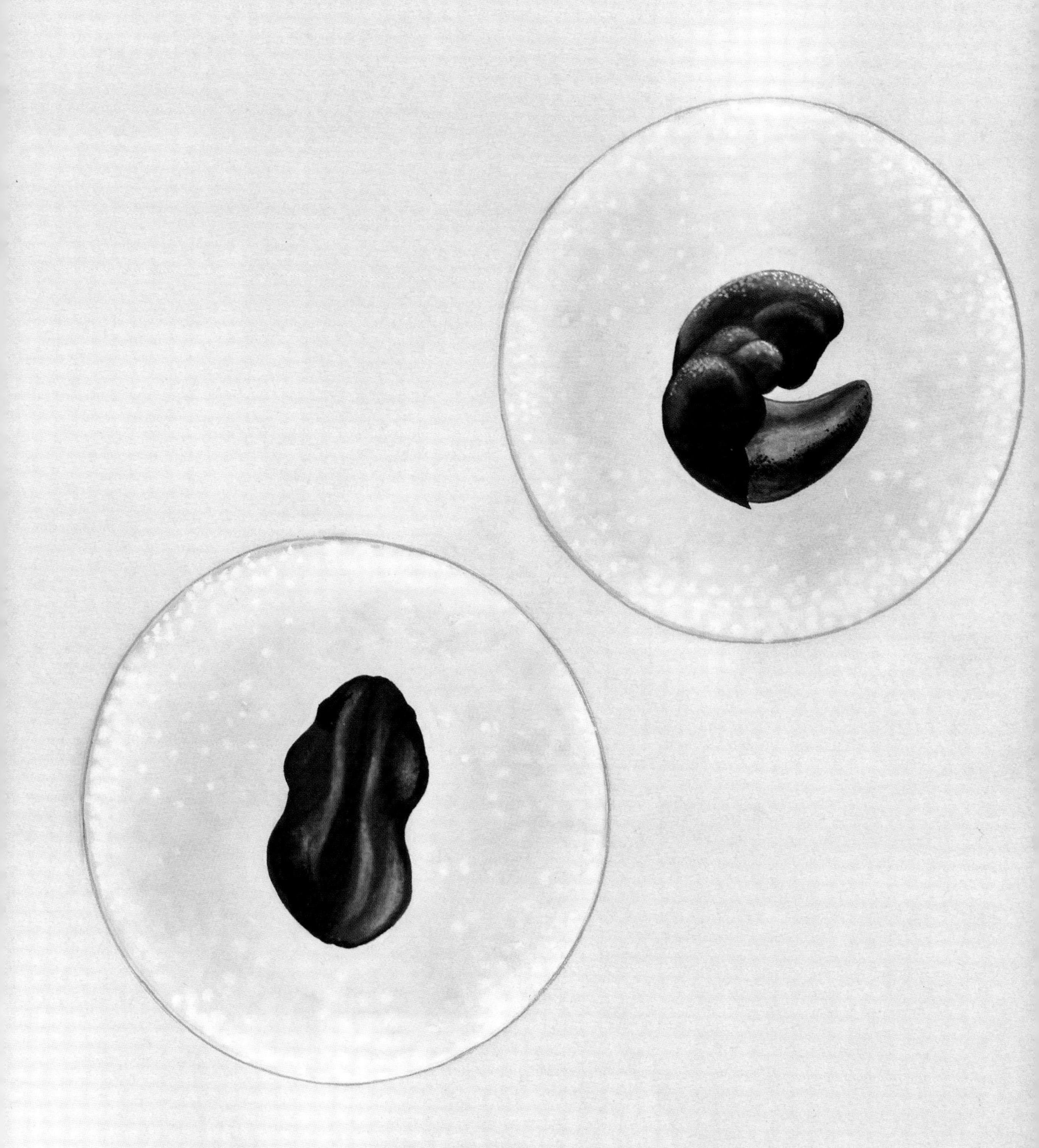

# The tadpoles hatch out of the jelly balls.

After about ten days the tadpoles are ready to **hatch** out. They wriggle and wriggle until they are out of the jelly balls. Only a few will live long enough to become frogs. Many are eaten by fish.

# The tadpoles swim in the water.

Can you see the feathery things on each side of the tadpole's head? These are called the **gills**. Tadpoles need gills so that they can **breathe** under the water.

# The tadpoles begin to grow.

When tadpoles are very young they eat small water plants. As they grow bigger they can eat small water animals. The tadpoles still have their gills but now they are tucked inside the skin.

# The tadpoles grow back legs.

At last the tadpoles begin to grow back legs. It is seven weeks since they hatched from their eggs. They have also grown **lungs** inside their bodies. Now they have to come up to the surface and breathe the air through their mouths.

# The back legs grow bigger.

The tadpoles still need their tails to swim. The front legs are now growing under the skin where the gills used to be. Can you see the bulges where the front legs are growing?

# The tadpoles have four legs.

Look at these two tadpoles. It is twelve weeks since they hatched. They have four legs. They will soon start to use them. Only the back ones are used for swimming. Can you see the long toes on the back feet?

# The tail begins to shrink.

Look again. The tadpole's tail is getting shorter. Can you see the **webs** between the toes on the back feet? These help the frog to swim quickly.

# The young frogs climb out of the pond.

Young frogs are called froglets. Of course they are very tiny – only about the size of a thimble! They begin to look for food. They use their long sticky tongues to catch insects and tiny animals.

# The tiny frogs grow up.

Slowly, the frogs grow up to look like their parents. After three years the females will lay their eggs in a pond. What do you think will happen then?

# Keeping your own tadpoles.

Only collect from ponds that have a lot of frogspawn. Do not put tadpoles in new tap water. Leave the water in a tank for two days. Put clean sand and stones in the tank. Remember, one large stone must be higher than the water. Put in fresh water plants and a water snail. These will keep the water clean.

When they are very small tadpoles will eat the plants. When they grow bigger they will eat meat. Hang a small piece of meat in the water. Do not keep it there long because it will make the water dirty. When they have grown front legs they will climb out of the water. Now return them to their pond.

# The life cycle of a frog.

How many stages of the life cycle can you remember?

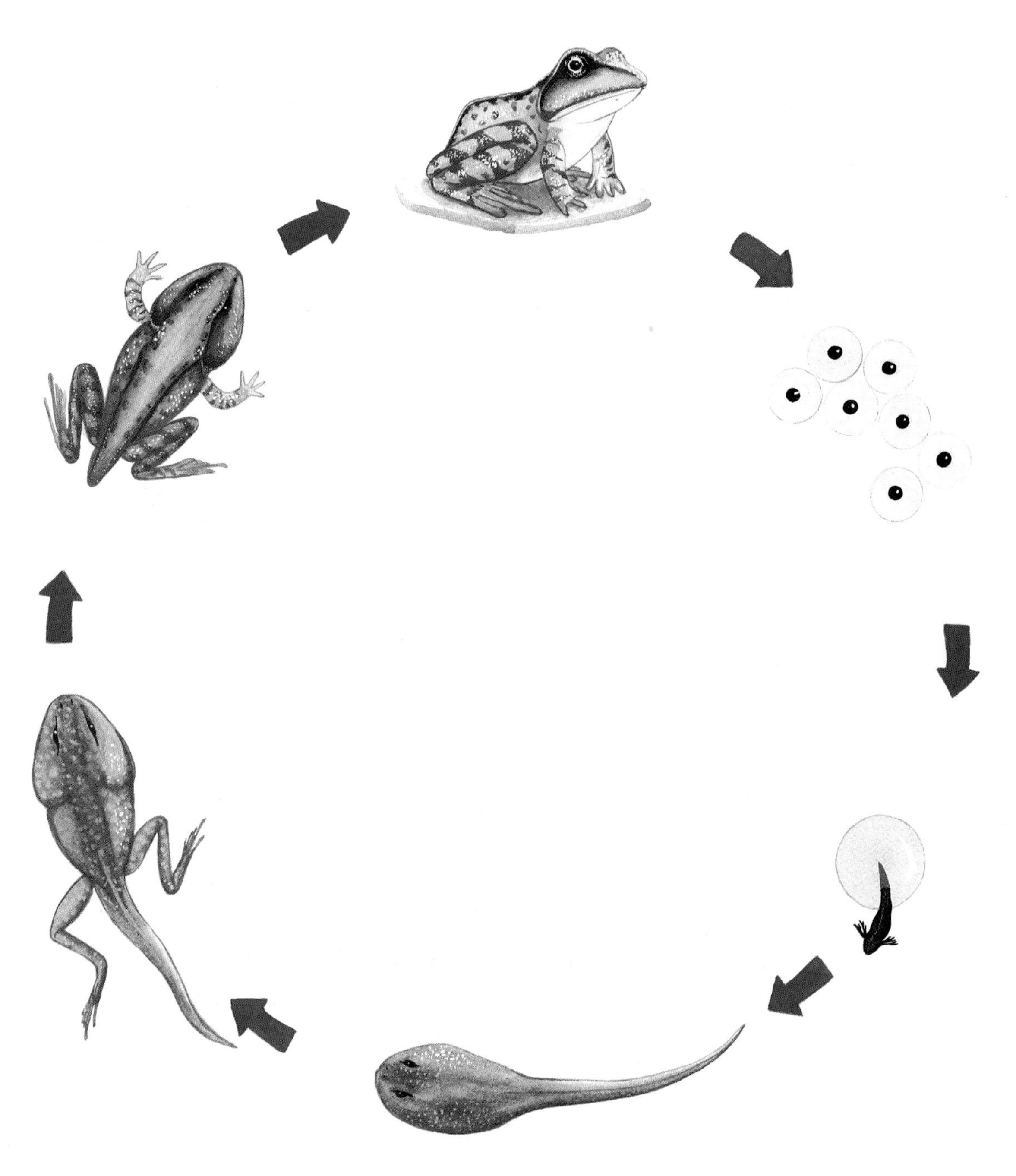

# Glossary

**Amphibian** An animal that starts life in water but later can move on land. Some, like frogs, will grow up and spend a lot of time on the land.

**Breathe** To take fresh air into the body and to give stale air out. All animals need air to live.

**Frogspawn** The hundreds of growing eggs are called frogspawn. They stick together and float to the top of the pond.

**Gills** All animals that breathe under water need gills. Gills help them take air from the water.

**Hatch** To break out of an egg.

**Lungs** Animals that breathe air like we do need lungs. Lungs are air bags which are inside the body of the animal.

**Mate** This is when male (father) and female (mother) animals join together. This is how a baby animal is made.

**Sperm** This is the liquid from the male frog which mixes with the female's eggs. If this does not happen the eggs will not grow into young frogs.

**Tadpoles** These are the little animals that hatch out of the frog's eggs.

**Webs** These are pieces of skin stretched between the toes. They help in swimming.

# Finding out more

Here are some books to read to find out more.

*Animals and their Young* by Malcolm Penny (Wayland, 1987)
*Animal Movement* by Malcolm Penny (Wayland, 1987)
*Discovering Frogs and Toads* by Mike Linley (Wayland, 1986)
*The Frog* by Margaret Lane (Methuen, 1981)
*Frogs and Toads* by Kate Petty (Franklin Watts, 1985)
*In the Pond* by Sarah McKenzie (Wayland, 1985)
*The Tree Frog* (Wayland, 1979)

# Index